THE
BOOK OF
BRILLIANCE

....

A Story
For Everyone Who
Wants to Have a Little
Smile About Their Truth

....

WELCOME TO YOUR JOURNEY

We are born with a lightness, children from the beginning. And if we're not careful, we can get way too serious about being "adults." My hope is that you find a place within, where your precious spark – your lightness – becomes real to you always, and that you remember the grace and brilliance of being you without ever having to try.

Introduction

We are the explorers of our lives, travelers searching for the common truths found in our human experience. We question our lives, search for a clarity of purpose, and strive to know our own hearts. It's a shared journey we all live together – this life of discovering who we're designed to be. And *The Book of Brilliance* offers us permission to open those doors of self-awareness a bit wider; permission to reach for and touch that unique and internal wisdom found in everyone. It helps us create a path in life that offers us greater capacity to live from the heart, and to know a deeper self-love.

In a sense, *The Book of Brilliance* helps us heal a part of ourselves by providing a simple path toward reclaiming our truest identity. Whispering its words touches lives, including our own. It helps us make use of the enormous resources found in being human and points us toward a deeper and more abundant life. We simply need to give ourselves permission to accept the gifts within us, while also learning to prosper in them. *The Book of Brilliance* helps us touch that heart-centered journey.

Try this. Offer these next phrases in part or in whole to the friends and family you interact with and watch their response. **Let them know that: "They are lovable, precious, valuable, and one-of-a-kind unique in this world. They make a difference, they're enough just as they are, worthy of being, and they simply belong here."** The stories you'll gain from the experience will impact you. It's profound when we use these words with healthy intention. They very naturally impact everyone involved. You might get a quizzical look at first, but deep down, you're sparking a truth we've all known, and many have waited their whole life to hear it. Whether it's offered to somebody with dementia, someone abused as a child, or simply to a loved one, these words hold power, and they're meant for all of us. So, use them well, and use them freely, because they give the world permission to heal and change.

A special note to the reader:

Whether you're a parent, grandparent, spouse, partner, sibling, or friend, take your time with the words and the truth held in this book. As you quietly explore, read its phrases many times to yourself. And in a personal way, try to embody its deep message before sharing it with someone you love. Because when we know a truth personally, it helps us teach it in a more profound way.

And as you read, let yourself occasionally pause when you need, so you can affirm or reinforce a particular truth, relate a meaningful story, or simply clarify the gift someone is in your life, including yourself. This is where you become "that person," that special heart-centered friend that helped another touch their inner wisdom and remember the preciousness of their existence. This is where you become a gift to another's life.

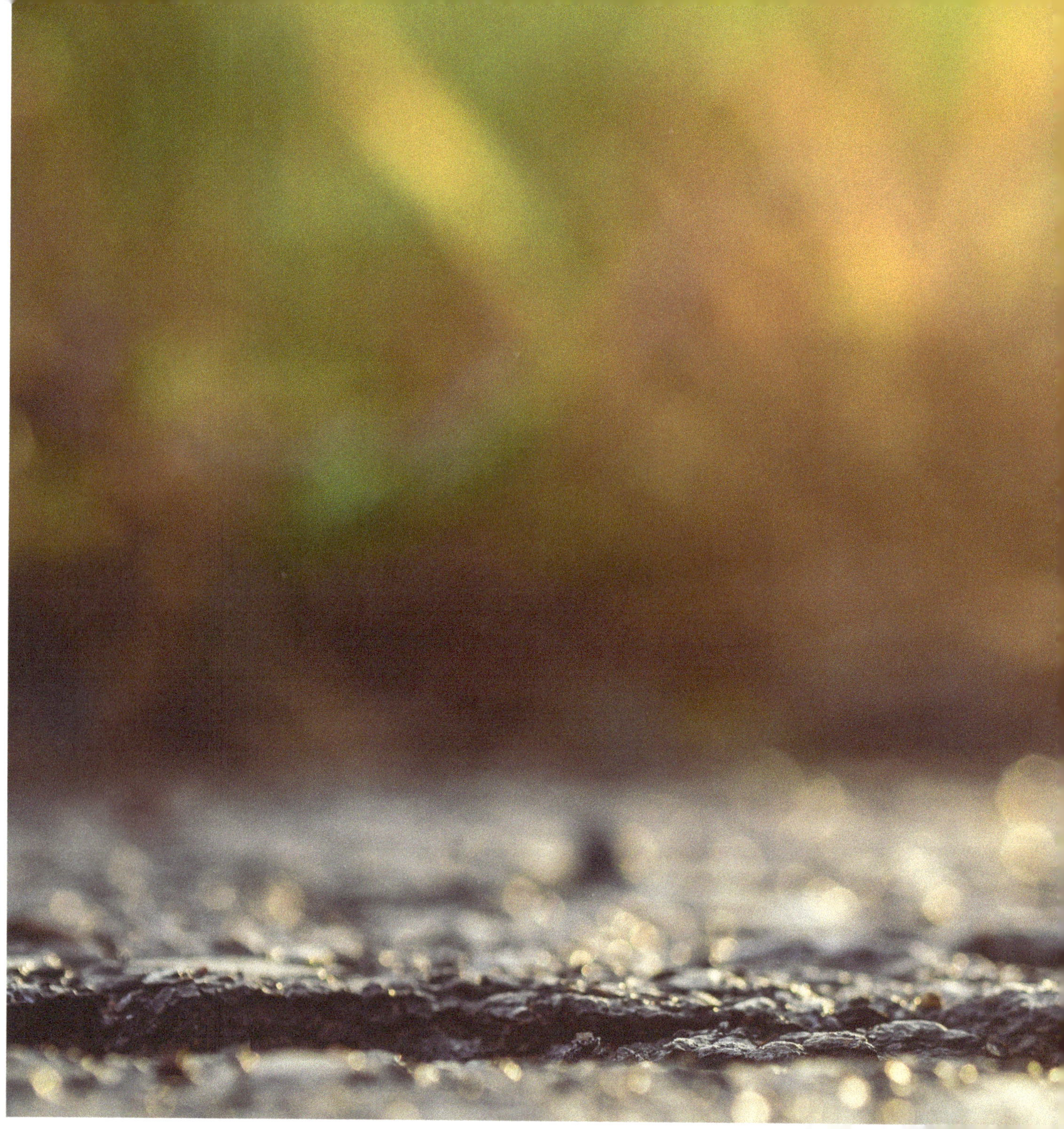

There's a Brilliance you bring,
    a Uniqueness that's all yours.

YES, YOU

You are a wonder. Lovable, simply because you are you.

Precious, just as you are.

You hold a value and a worth that's beyond measure, simply because you exist.

And your presence, the very fact that you're alive, makes a difference to this world.

You're unique, one of a kind. There has never been another you, and there never will be.

Your presence in this world is a priceless gift, incomparable in its value.

There's simply no replacement for what you bring to this world.

And everything you need has already been placed within you.

You're already enough, just as you are.

And from the moment you became real, you were perfect.

You were made for this world, and you absolutely belong here just as you are.

So live your life, let yourself grow in the direction of your own heart,

and open to the lessons held within this life that are unfolding to you every moment.

Whisper these simple words to yourself,

> I am lovable.
>
> I am precious.
>
> I am valuable.
>
> I am unique.
>
> I make a difference.
>
> I am enough.
>
> I am worthy.
>
> I belong.

And know that they are always true.

Feel them all, one at a time.
Let them touch your heart,
so you can always hold them close.

THEY WAKE UP A LIGHT ALREADY WITHIN YOU.

Because this is the language of the heart,
where we all find our truth...

When life is easy,
and especially when it feels most difficult,
speak these words to yourself.

I am lovable.
I am precious.
I am valuable.
I am unique.
I make a difference.
I am enough.
I am worthy.
I belong.

Let them move through you,
    and let them dance bravely within you.
And allow yourself to become a wondrous partner with your life.

Wake up to the
BEAUTIFUL MIRACLE
of knowing that you

are strong, awake, and alive...

..and that you are made to be
CREATIVE

LIVE BEYOND

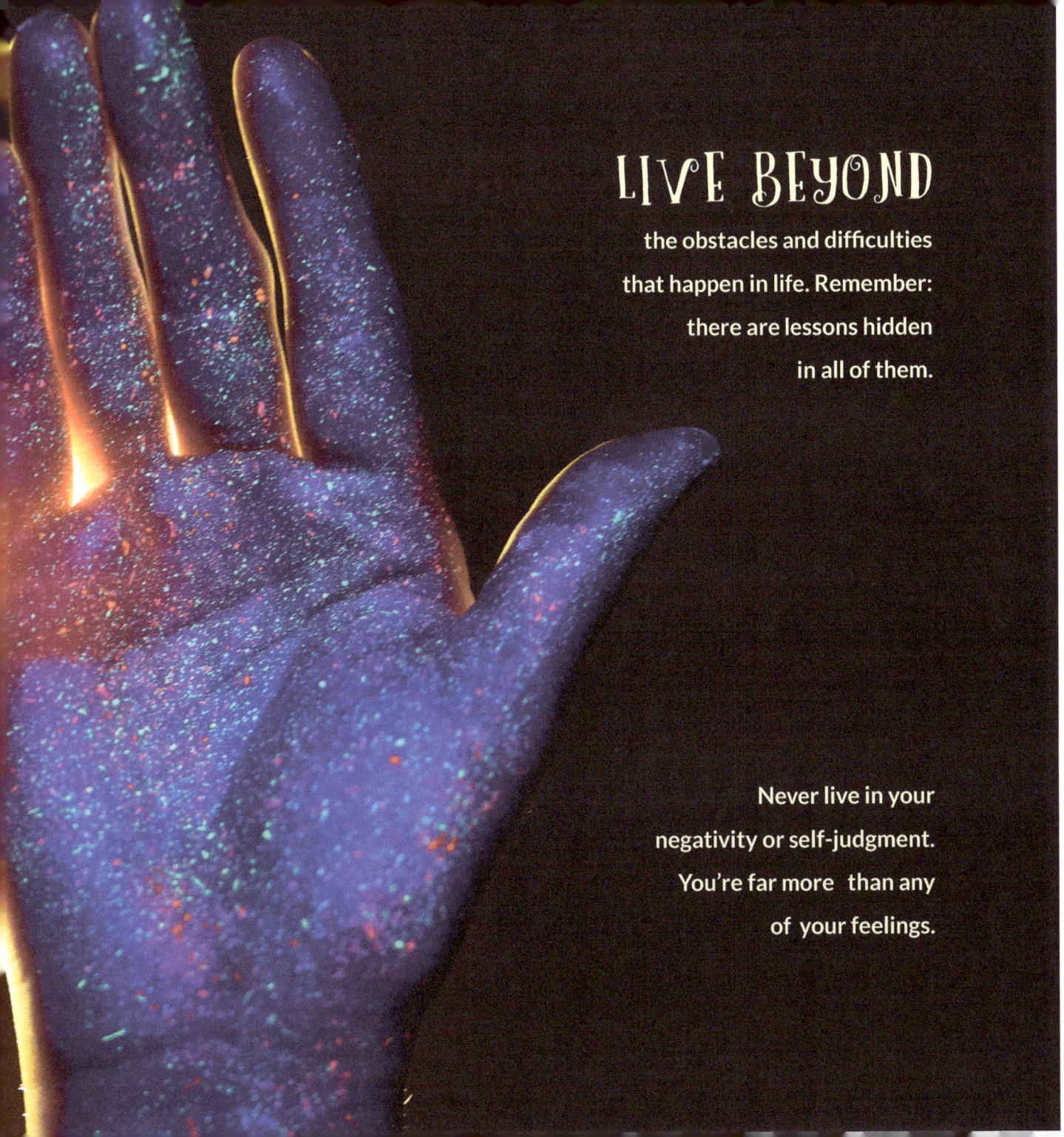

the obstacles and difficulties that happen in life. Remember: there are lessons hidden in all of them.

Never live in your negativity or self-judgment. You're far more than any of your feelings.

Fear and anxiety don't get to blaze the trails of your world.

YOU DO.

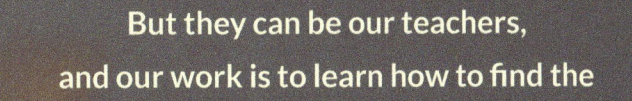

But they can be our teachers,
and our work is to learn how to find the

WISDOM

they hold.

Sometimes our lessons take a while,
so stay open and be

PATIENT

as you learn.

And as you live your life,

FREE YOURSELF TO GROW...

and never stop.

YOU'RE CREATED TO THRIVE,

designed with the purpose
of becoming your best you.

Let yourself blossom wherever you are.

You're meant to share yourself with the world, to open up un-shy and to reach for life with an astonished amazement.

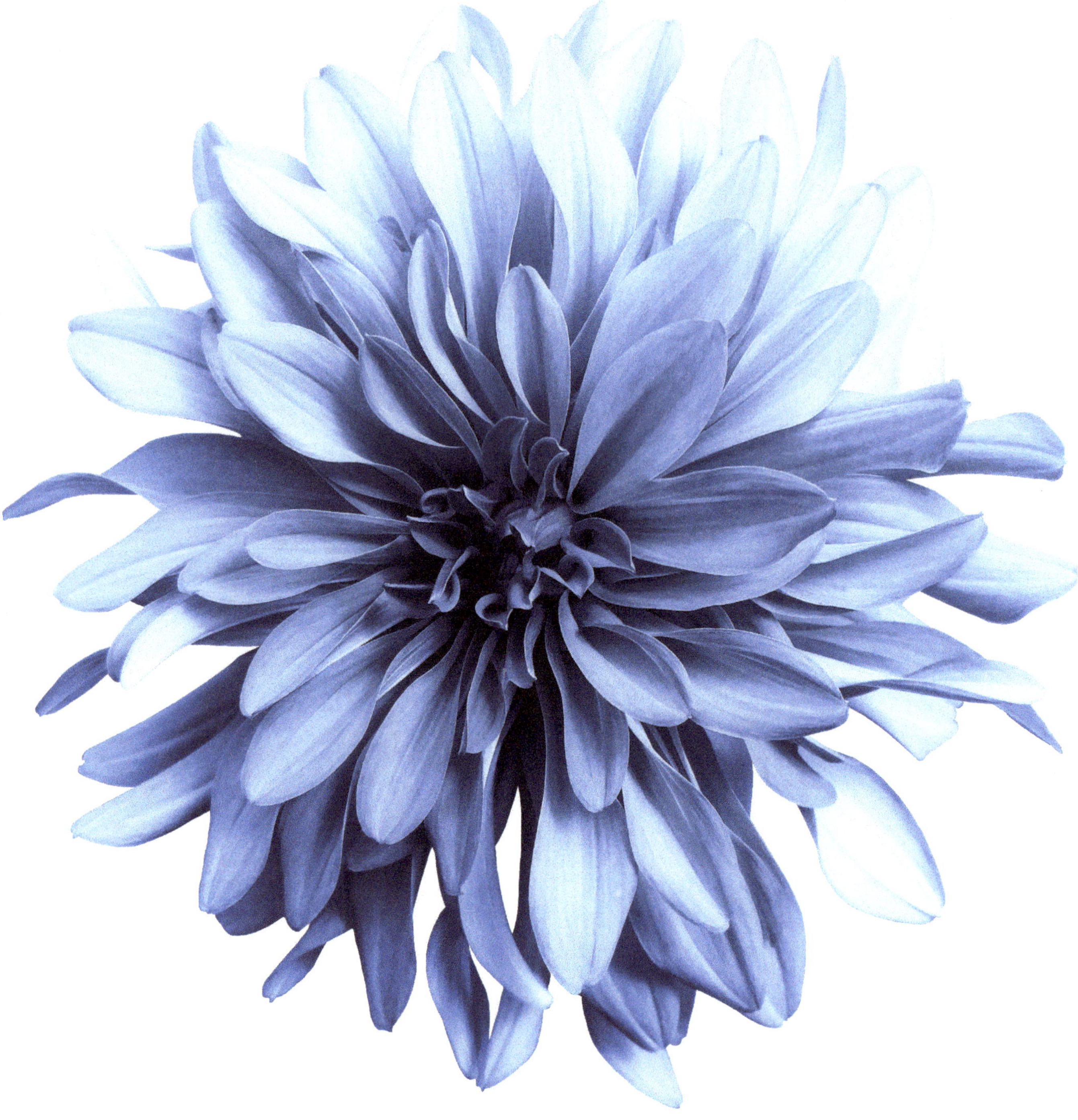

You're like a flower in this world.

And a flower can only be what it is... a flower.

It grows in the most difficult places, and

BLOSSOMS

in the muddiest of waters.

And you are no different.

YOU'RE DESIGNED TO THRIVE,

to grow regardless of where you are.

And you, just like that flower,

you're created to

BLOSSOM

precisely into yourself.

Strong and capable,

CURIOUS
AND CREATIVE,

awake and alive.

YOU CAN CHOOSE
the life that you want to create.

YOU CAN CHOOSE
what you want to set aside.

And only your own thinking

can hold you back.

SO BE FREE, BE YOU.

Offer your brilliance to the world.

**Wake up to the wonder
of what your self-love and
self-acceptance can accomplish.**

And then explore all that life holds for you.

LET YOURSELF CREATE,
LET YOURSELF EXPAND,

let yourself thrive in this life.

Open yourself up to the magic held within

the beauty of your wondrous unfolding world.

And yes… absolutely. No matter what…

You are lovable.

You are precious.

You are valuable.

You are unique.

You make a difference.

You are enough.

You are worthy.

AND YOU ALWAYS, ALWAYS BELONG.

And when you can see

the precious brilliance that you are,

it helps you see it in everyone.

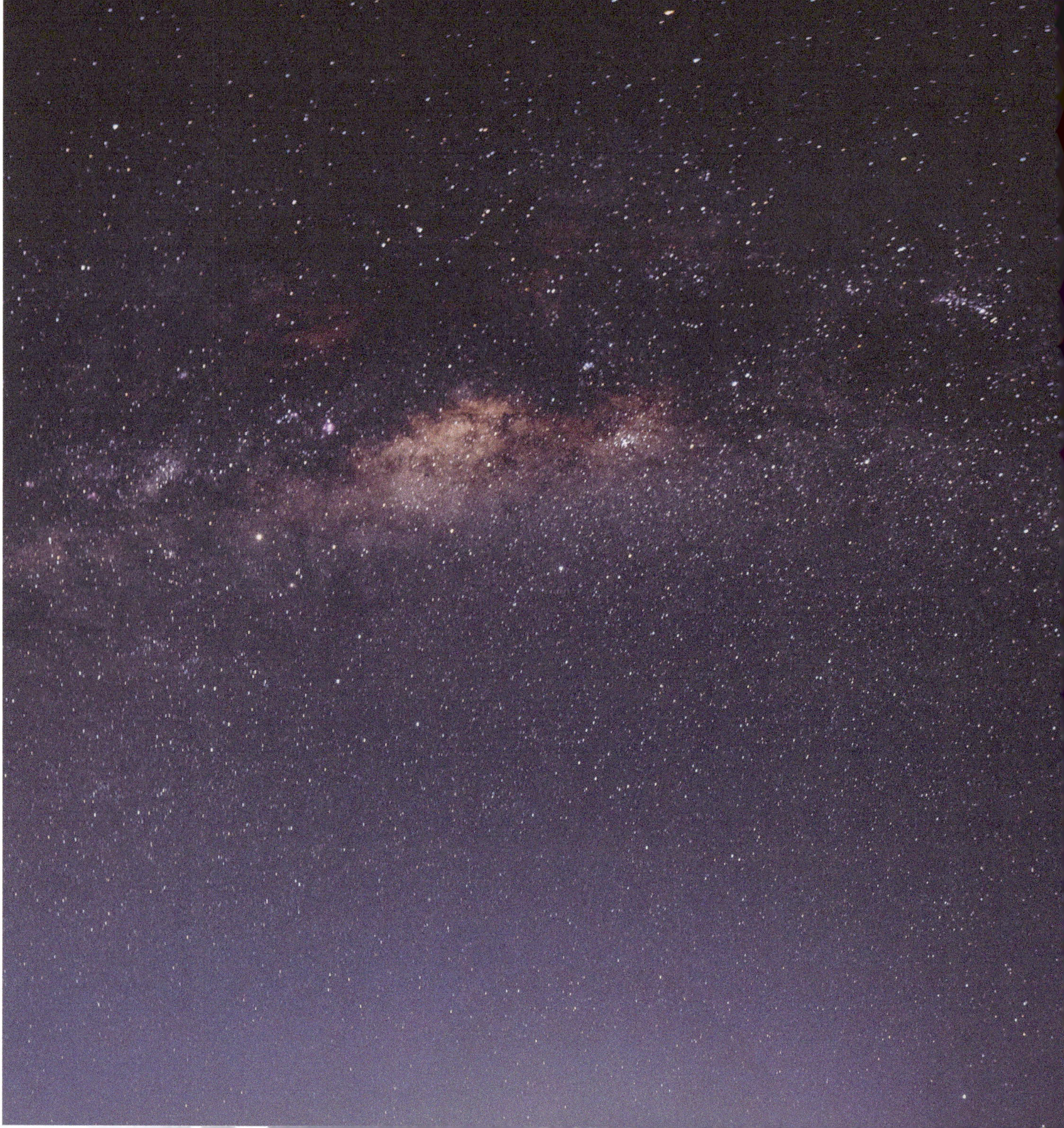

So, welcome to your life,

WELCOME TO YOUR WONDERFUL JOURNEY.

And remember, whatever you choose to nurture in your life will grow.

LITTLE BANNERS

You're lovable, and sooo precious. Valuable beyond measure, and entirely unique in your own special way.

You make a difference in this world, just being you.

You belong here, and you make "here" even more special.

Please feel free to copy these pages and cut them out so that you can share these little banners with the people who you feel could use a little reminder about their truth.

Be all your wondrous wonders, and dance with your life. Become alive as only you can, and share yourself with the world.

You're unique, special in a way only you can be, and the only one that can be the wonderful that you are. There's only one fantastimungus you!

I am lovable.
I am precious.
I am valuable.
I am unique.
I make a difference.
I am enough.
I am worthy.
I belong.

Please feel free to copy these pages and cut them out so that you can share these little banners with the people who you feel could use a little reminder about their truth.

Remember, Remember, Remember:
You are pure brilliance. A precious spark
of life, unique in your special way.

You bring brilliance to this life.
You fire up the "sparkly"
of being alive.

You're precious and spectacular,
and being yourself is your
amazing gift to the world.

You are lovable.

You are precious.

You are valuable.

You are
beautifully unique.

You make a difference.

You are enough.

You are
wonderfully worthy.

You genuinely belong here,

no if ands or butts about it.

Please feel free to copy these pages and cut them out so that you can share these little banners with the people who you feel could use a little reminder about their truth.

What a gift you bring to this world.
So precious, strong and wise. This world is
lucky that your wonderful self exists.

Bring your unique sparks of you to the
world, and in your own special way you
touch the hearts of the people around you.

You're a spectacular, marvelous, and
razzly-dazzly one of a kind human!
You're the perfect expression of you!

About the Author
Brian Roscoe

Dr. Roscoe enjoys writing about the journey of life, discovering the unique wisdom within all of us, and helping people create a life based in self-love. He loves hiking, biking, nature photography, and exploring the mysteries human nature holds. Dr. Roscoe also operates a holistic chiropractic clinic, working with patients in releasing physical injury and stress, as well as emotional attachments that limit their life expression. *The Book of Brilliance* is a culmination of the message he teaches and is written for people of all ages.

To purchase any of Brian's titles in bulk or to connect with Brian:
BrianRoscoeAuthor.com
brianroscoe61@gmail.com
(616) 847-1444

CONTINUE THE JOURNEY
books by Brian

Inspirational Espresso

Get your daily shot of inspiration! In his book, Inspirational Espresso, Dr. Brian Roscoe walks us through the importance of looking inward and questioning ourselves in the interest of cultivating a higher state of wellbeing and, therefore, a richer life experience. With little shots of wisdom guiding you to question your motives, integrity, and direction, Brian helps pave the way for choosing to learn to love better while maintaining a sense of compassion, understanding, and truth towards yourself and all others.

"Our purpose here in this wildly marvelous world is to remember how to expand into a place of deep, multilayered, unconditional love – a love that is, in essence, who we already are and have always been."

Inspirational Espresso will leave hints of truth, inspire moments of wisdom and understanding, as well as mindfully helping us live our lives pointed toward a gentler, more compassionate way while immersed in this fantastic journey of living.

Call of the Heart: Six Secrets to Self-Love

CALL OF THE HEART is the gateway to your journey back to yourself. Roscoe presents a journey guided by love and self-discovery that will change your perspective on life, forgiveness, relationships, and your journey's purpose.

In this book, you will find:

- guidance and inspiration for living through love
- how to discover your inner worth and light
- how to see the gifts in your wounds
- introspective prompts to carry you along the journey
- Listen to the call of your heart, and journey through this book to uncover the six secrets to self-love.

Call of the Heart, Awakened: The Journey of Self-Love

CALL OF THE HEART, in its second installment, takes readers deeply into the journey of self-love. Using all of the insights and tools of the first Call of the Heart book, Awakened steps into the minds and aspirations of everyone who explores its pages, helping them see an enlightened way—the truth within themselves.

In this book, you will find:

- a deep dive into what it means to live with self-love
- how to manifest your inner gifts
- how to elevate your perspective
- introspective prompts to carry you along the journey
- Listen to the call of your heart, and journey more deeply into the remembering of your spirited self.

Power Statement Logbook: Mentoring the Habits of the Heart

THE POWER STATEMENT LOGBOOK is a companion guide to the Call of the Heart series. This workbook empowers readers to take charge of their journey by guiding them through meditations and musings on how to find, harness, and employ your personal power every single day.

In this book, you will find:

- deeper insights into the journey of self-love
- prompts to help stir your inner wanderer
- activities for introspection and growth
- guidance and tips for your journey ahead
- Listen to the call of your heart, and journey more deeply into your personal power.

The New-Now: The Art of Being Right Here, Right Now

We're here to activate a higher consciousness from within to reclaim our own miracle. Our journey was designed to be an inspired one, one we're all meant to embrace, and it's expressed through the gift of a world that infinitely unfolds into each unique life. So welcome. Welcome to your life. Welcome to the journey.

Are you ready to fully engage mindfulness?

Are you ready to honor each and every moment?

Are you ready for a new perspective?

Welcome to the New-Now.

PLEASE LEAVE A REVIEW

Public reviews help independent authors bring you the books you love. If you loved this book, please leave a review on Amazon. You can also leave your feedback on social media by connecting with Brian @drbrianroscoe. Thank you! And enjoy your journey!

The Book of Brilliance: a story for everyone who wants to have a little smile about their truth
Copyright © 2021 by Brian Roscoe

All rights reserved. No part of this publication may be reproduced, distributed, or transmitted in any form or by any means, including photocopying, recording, or other electronic or mechanical methods, without the prior written permission of the author, except in the case of brief quotations embodied in critical reviews and certain other noncommercial uses permitted by copyright law.

Neither the author, publisher, nor any of their employees or representatives guarantees the accuracy of information in this book or its usefulness to a particular reader, nor are they responsible for any damage or negative consequence that may result from any treatment, action taken, or inaction by any person reading or following the information in this book.

For permission requests or to contact the author, visit: brianroscoeauthor.com

ISBN-13: 978-1-957348-13-1

Printed in the United States of America

Printed in the USA
CPSIA information can be obtained
at www.ICGtesting.com
CBHW081401271123
2154CB00001B/4